ORGANIC FERTILIZER PRODUCTION FOR BEGINNERS

EASY GUIDE

A Quick Guide For Novice Gardeners On Creating Sustainable, Nutrient-Rich Soil From Scratch

WAYLEN BANNARD

CHAPTER ONE
ORGANIC FERTILIZERS

In modern agricultural techniques, the idea of producing organic fertilizer is quite important, especially when it comes to improving soil health. Because they come from natural sources, organic fertilizers are essential for advancing sustainable agriculture. Organic fertilizers, as opposed to chemical fertilizers, increase soil fertility without hurting the environment. In this talk, the fundamentals of producing organic fertilizer are discussed, along with the development of the product and its many advantages over chemical alternatives.

Recognizing The Significance Of Soil Health

A key factor in determining both agricultural output and the sustainability of ecosystems is soil health. The complex interactions between biological, chemical, and physical elements in the soil matrix affect the soil's general health. Due to their potential to improve soil structure, promote healthy soil microbiota, and increase nutrient availability, organic fertilizers are essential for maintaining soil health. The soil's ability to retain water, breathe, and drain better when organic matter is added by organic fertilizers. Thus, a robust and productive soil ecology is ensured, encouraging ideal root development and nutrient uptake by plants.

The Development Of The Production Of Organic Fertilizer:

The early realization of the drawbacks and environmental effects of chemical fertilizers is credited with the development of organic fertilizer production. As agriculture evolved from traditional ways to more intensive operations, the adverse impacts of synthetic fertilizers on soil health and the environment became apparent. This insight led to the creation of organic fertilizer production techniques that follow the guidelines of sustainable agriculture. The development of organic farming methods, waste recycling, and technology over time has improved the efficiency and scalability of the procedures used to produce organic fertilizers. The development of organic fertilizer production, from basic composting procedures to complex bioconversion processes, demonstrates a comprehensive strategy for soil health and environmental sustainability.

Advantages Of Using Organic Fertilizers Rather Than Chemicals:

Choosing organic fertilizers over chemical ones has several advantages for the environment, agriculture, and human health. By promoting long-term soil fertility and lowering the possibility of nutrient runoff into water bodies, organic fertilizers gradually release nutrients into the soil. This guarantees a more sustainable nutrient cycle throughout the ecosystem in addition to reducing water pollution. Furthermore, organic fertilizers increase the amount of organic matter in the soil, which promotes biodiversity and microbial activity. Encouraging a symbiotic relationship between soil microbes and plants increases plant resilience and helps reduce disease. Additionally, the possibility of chemical residues in food crops is eliminated by the absence of synthetic chemicals in organic fertilizers, protecting human health and lessening the environmental impact of conventional agriculture.

To sum up, the creation and application of organic fertilizers stand out as an essential step toward achieving sustainable agriculture. A thorough understanding of the role of organic fertilizers in promoting agricultural and environmental sustainability requires an understanding of the significance of soil health, the history of organic fertilizer production, and the numerous advantages of selecting organic alternatives. A harmonious relationship between agriculture and the ecosystem can only be fostered by embracing organic fertilizers as we negotiate the challenges of modern agriculture.

CHAPTER TWO

FOUNDATIONS OF SOIL HEALTH

Understanding the complex composition and structure of soil is the first step toward maintaining soil health. Soil is a complex mixture of air, water, organic matter, and mineral particles. The three types of mineral particles—clay, silt, and sand—determine the texture of the soil.

Clay particles are smaller and have finer grains than sand particles, which are bigger and coarser. Particles of silt settle in between. The arrangement of these particles affects the porosity, water retention, and aeration capacity of the soil by changing its structural makeup. The availability of nutrients, water infiltration, and root penetration—all essential elements for plant growth—are enhanced by a healthy soil structure.

Microbial Life in the Soil: Improving soil health greatly depends on the existence of microorganisms in the soil.

Protozoa, nematodes, fungi, bacteria, and other microorganisms abound in the rich and dynamic ecosystem that is the soil. These microscopic creatures aid in the decomposition of organic debris, the cycling of nutrients, and the prevention of disease. For example, symbiotic connections between mycorrhizal fungus and plant roots enable better nutrient uptake. Organic stuff is transformed into forms that plants can use by bacteria. Producing organic fertilizers requires an understanding of the dynamics of microbial communities since these fertilizers have the power to either promote or inhibit microbial activity, which in turn affects the general health of the soil.

pH Levels and Nutrient Availability: One important aspect affecting a plant's ability to get nutrients is the pH level of the soil. The neutral pH is 7.0, and the pH scale goes from acidic to alkaline. Most plants grow best in neutral to slightly acidic soils. The solubility of minerals is impacted by the pH of the soil, which impacts the availability of vital nutrients.

For example, alkaline soils can cause nutritional deficits, while acidic soils frequently result in aluminum and manganese toxicity. Organic fertilizers can affect soil pH through their decomposition processes. It is important to maintain a pH balance to maximize plant uptake of nutrients, hence organic fertilizers must be carefully designed to support this balance without significantly altering soil pH.

Improving Soil Health By Producing Organic Fertilizers

The comprehension of nutrient content and release dynamics is a crucial element in the development of organic fertilizers. The nutrients in organic fertilizers come from organic materials including plant leftovers, dung, and compost. As these components break down, nutrients are progressively released into the soil. In contrast to their synthetic counterparts, which frequently have more immediate nutrient availability, organic fertilizers have different nutrient-release kinetics. Organic fertilizers have a slow-release characteristic that corresponds with the natural rate at which plants absorb nutrients, so fostering continuous development without creating nutritional imbalances or seeping into groundwater.

Composting Procedures and Microbial Activation: A lot of the processes used to produce organic fertilizers revolve around the composting process. By breaking down organic waste under regulated circumstances, composting produces an end product that is high in nutrients. The final fertilizer's microbial activation is greatly influenced by the composting methods selected. For instance, aerobic composting encourages the development of advantageous fungi and bacteria, supporting a thriving microbial community. Organic fertilizers have a microbial activity that increases nutrient availability and transformation, promoting plant development while inhibiting dangerous diseases.

Maintaining a Balanced Nutrient Profile: When producing organic fertilizer, maintaining a balanced nutrient profile is essential. Organic fertilizers frequently have variable nutrient contents, in contrast to synthetic fertilizers that could have precise, predetermined nutritional ratios. To create organic fertilizers that balance potassium, phosphorus, and nitrogen levels while also including other vital micronutrients, a meticulous selection of raw materials is necessary. To avoid negative impacts on plant growth and to preserve the general health of the soil, nutrient imbalances must be avoided. To create organic fertilizers that are effective and meet particular agricultural needs, it is essential to understand the nutrient requirements of the target crops.

Reducing Environmental Impact: By reducing environmental impact, the manufacturing of organic fertilizer is in line with sustainable agriculture. Organic fertilizers, in contrast to synthetic ones, come from renewable resources and are frequently a consequence of different agricultural processes. The use of organic fertilizers lowers the possibility of nutrient runoff, a factor in water contamination. Furthermore, the gradual release characteristic of organic fertilizers reduces the possibility of overfertilization, averting the build-up of surplus nutrients in the soil. This environmentally friendly method helps to conserve the environment more broadly while also promoting soil health.

Integration with Crop Rotation and Cover Cropping: Strategic agricultural techniques like crop rotation and cover cropping, in addition to the application of organic fertilizers, are part of an integrated approach to soil health. Crop rotation enhances soil fertility and structure while severing pest and disease cycles. When used with organic fertilizers, cover crops improve soil organic matter, inhibit weed growth, and improve water retention. The generation of organic fertilizer and these farming methods work in concert to promote long-term sustainability and resilience in agroecosystems by encouraging a holistic approach to soil health.

In conclusion, producing organic fertilizer effectively requires an awareness of the basic principles of soil health, such as pH levels, microbial life, and soil makeup. Organic fertilizers guarantee soil health since they focus on nutritional content, ratios of nutrients, composting methods, and environmental impact. Organic fertilizers are essential for building robust and fruitful agroecosystems when combined with sustainable agriculture methods. This all-encompassing strategy benefits the planet's health and our food systems' long-term sustainability in addition to increasing agricultural output today.

CHAPTER THREE

TYPES OF ORGANIC MATERIALS FOR FERTILIZER PRODUCTION

Plant-Based Substances:

Plant-based ingredients are necessary for the manufacturing of organic fertilizers, which improve soil health. These materials come from a variety of sources, such as plant byproducts, green manures, and crop wastes. Straw and stalks are examples of crop wastes that are high in carbon and give organic fertilizers their structural support. On the other hand, to increase the fertility of the soil, green manures entail the cultivation and inclusion of particular plants. For example, legume plants are essential for fixing nitrogen, which is a necessary ingredient for plant growth. Furthermore, residual plant materials and vegetable waste add to the organic matter content of fertilizers, improving their nutritious profile. The use of plant-based materials highlights how sustainable the manufacturing of organic fertilizer is because it encourages recycling and lessens reliance on artificial inputs.

Animal-Based Content:

Another important area in the manufacturing of organic fertilizers is materials derived from animals. These components, which come from animal sources, are essential to the production of fertilizers that are high in nutrients. Livestock manure, from pigs, chickens, and cows, is a major source of organic matter and important nutrients like phosphate and nitrogen. Animal feces break down and form humus, which enhances soil structure and retention of water. Furthermore, animal-based products that increase the nutritious content of organic fertilizers include fish emulsion, blood meal, and bones. By addressing both organic matter and nutrient deficits, the use of these materials guarantees a comprehensive approach to improving soil health and offers a sustainable option for waste management in the agricultural industry.

Methods For Composting:

A key step in the creation of organic fertilizer is composting, which is the carefully regulated breakdown of organic waste to produce a humus that is rich in nutrients. This method encourages the balanced, slow release of vital nutrients, which is crucial for improving soil health. There are two types of composting processes: aerobic and anaerobic. Each kind affects the properties of the finished organic fertilizer. To promote aeration and reduce odors, aerobic composting uses the activity of microorganisms that are dependent on oxygen to break down organic materials. Anaerobic composting, on the other hand, happens without oxygen and produces organic acids as well as perhaps unpleasant odors. To maximize the quality of organic fertilizers, one must comprehend the complexities of these composting methods.

The temperature, moisture content, and carbon-to-nitrogen ratio are other important variables that affect how well the composting process works. By using appropriate composting methods, high-quality organic fertilizers that support sustainable agricultural practices and improved soil health can be produced.

To summarize, the manufacture of organic fertilizers to improve soil health is based on the use of materials derived from plants and animals as well as efficient composting methods. These methods increase soil structure, water retention, and microbial activity overall in addition to addressing nutrient inadequacies. Organic fertilizer manufacturing is sustainable since it is based on recycling and waste use, which is in line with ecologically balanced and environmentally friendly agricultural principles.

CHAPTER FOUR

ESSENTIAL NUTRIENTS IN ORGANIC FERTILIZERS

Organic fertilizers are vital for improving soil health since they supply vital nutrients required for plant development. Understanding and incorporating essential nutrients—nitrogen, phosphorus, and potassium (NPK) in particular—is one of the core ideas in the production of organic fertilizer. A vital component of proteins, amino acids, and chlorophyll, nitrogen is necessary for the growth and development of plants. Compost, manure, and cover crops are common organic sources of nitrogen used in organic fertilizers. Nitrogen from organic sources is released gradually, reducing the chance of leaching and fostering sustainable nutrient availability.

Another essential ingredient that helps with DNA and RNA synthesis, energy storage, and transport in plants is phosphorus.

Fish bone meal, rock phosphate, and bone meal are examples of organic fertilizers high in phosphorus. These sources not only improve the soil's structure and deliver phosphorus, but they also encourage microbial activity. The third element in the NPK trio, potassium, is essential for water uptake, enzyme activity, and general plant health. Compost, wood ash, and kelp meal are examples of organic resources that give the soil potassium. An NPK ratio that is balanced is ensured by using organic fertilizers, which supports sustainable soil fertility and holistic plant nutrition.

Organic Fertilizers' Secondary And Micronutrient Content:

Organic fertilizers must contain secondary and micronutrients in addition to NPK to provide a holistic strategy for improving soil health. Sulfur, calcium, and magnesium are examples of secondary nutrients that are essential to many plant physiological functions. For example, calcium is essential for the creation and structure of cell walls. Calcium can be found in fertilizers organically from sources like crushed eggshells and gypsum. Because magnesium is essential to the synthesis of chlorophyll, its presence in organic fertilizers guarantees the best possible photosynthetic activity. Compost and manure are good sources of sulfur, which is necessary for the synthesis of amino acids and enhances the general health of plants.

Micronutrients are similarly important for plant growth even if they are needed in lesser amounts. Micronutrients like iron, manganese, zinc, copper, boron, and molybdenum can be present in organic fertilizers. Every micronutrient serves a distinct purpose, such as hormone production or enzyme activation. For example, the formation of chlorophyll depends on iron, which is made available in the soil by organic sources such as compost and kelp meal.

A balanced supply of secondary and micronutrients is ensured by organic fertilizers by combining a variety of materials; this helps to prevent nutrient deficits and promotes optimal plant development.

Dynamics of Nutrient Release in Organic Fertilizers:

Using organic fertilizers effectively requires an understanding of the kinetics of nutrient release. Organic fertilizers distribute nutrients gradually, mimicking natural processes, in contrast to synthetic fertilizers. For plants to absorb nutrients and break down organic materials, microbial activity in the soil is essential. Temperature, moisture content, and the organic material's carbon-to-nitrogen ratio all affect how quickly nutrients are released. In addition to giving plants a steady supply of nutrients, this progressive release increases the variety and activity of soil microorganisms, improving the general health of the soil.

A crucial factor in the creation of organic fertilizers, the carbon-to-nitrogen (C: N) ratio affects the processes of nutrient release and breakdown. varied organic materials have varied optimum C: N ratios, and finding the correct balance is essential for effective nutrient cycling. Straw and wood chips are examples of materials with a high carbon content; on the other hand, manure and legume cover crops, which contain more nitrogen, have a lower C: N ratio. It is crucial to maintain a balance between these materials during the composting or fermentation process to prevent nitrogen immobilization or excess carbon, which can impede the availability of nutrients for plants.

Soil Health And Microbial Activity:

Because they stimulate microbial activity, organic fertilizers have a major positive impact on soil health. Microorganisms break down organic debris to release nutrients that are suitable for plant uptake. Microorganisms such as fungi, bacteria, and others are essential for disassembling complex chemical substances into simpler forms. This procedure enhances soil aeration, water retention, and structure in addition to releasing nutrients. Organic fertilizers promote a diversified microbial community that improves disease prevention and nutrient cycling, hence supporting a robust and long-lasting soil environment.

pH of Soil and Application of Organic Fertilizer:

One of the most important factors affecting the availability of nutrients to plants is the pH of the soil; the use of organic fertilizers can alter the pH of the soil in many ways. For example, the alkaline soil that results from adding materials like wood ash and lime to organic fertilizers can be raised. On the other hand, substances that lower soil pH, such as sulfur and acidic organic additions, can make the surrounding environment more acidic. Maintaining the ideal growing conditions for plants requires an understanding of how organic fertilizers affect the pH of the soil. Farmers and gardeners are better able to modify their applications of organic fertilizer to suit the unique requirements of various crops when they do routine soil tests and pH level monitoring.

Organic Manure and Sustainable Farming Practices:

The principles of sustainable agriculture are in line with the manufacture and application of organic fertilizers. Long-term environmental sustainability, biodiversity, and soil health are given top priority in organic farming operations. Farmers may help minimize pollution in the environment, enhance soil structure, and raise resistance to pests and illnesses by using organic fertilizers. By emphasizing the recycling of organic matter—compost, cover crops, and animal manure, for example—a closed nutrient cycle is further promoted, reducing the need for outside inputs. Adopting organic fertilizer techniques promotes a comprehensive and sustainable approach to agriculture and is both environmentally and financially sustainable over time.

Opportunities and Difficulties in the Production of Organic Fertilizer:

Although organic fertilizers have many advantages, there are difficulties in producing them. Achieving accurate nutrient formulations is hampered by the variations in nutrient concentration among various organic sources. Another issue is pathogen and weed seed contamination, which calls for appropriate fermentation and composting techniques. Furthermore, to address the unique nutritional requirements of plants, crop management strategies may need to be more sophisticated due to the slower nutrient release from organic fertilizers. Nonetheless, these difficulties offer chances for investigation and creativity in the manufacturing of organic fertilizers, such as the creation of standardized procedures, methods for ensuring quality, and cutting-edge nutrient-delivery systems.

To sum up, the process of producing organic fertilizer to improve soil health is centered on the assimilation of vital nutrients, comprehension of the dynamics of nutrient release, and stimulation of microbial activity. Comprehensive plant nutrition is ensured by a balanced supply of NPK, secondary nutrients, and micronutrients; the efficiency of nutrient release is influenced by the carbon-to-nitrogen ratio. The relationship between the pH of the soil and organic fertilizers, as well as the encouragement of microbial diversity, all support sustainable agricultural methods. Notwithstanding obstacles, using organic fertilizers is in line with sustainable agriculture and environmental stewardship principles, opening the door to a resilient and regenerative method of managing soil.

CHAPTER FIVE

METHODS FOR PRODUCING ORGANIC FERTILIZER

Vermicomposting, a famous organic fertilizer manufacturing process, involves the use of earthworms to break down organic waste into nutrient-rich compost. The capacity of this procedure to improve soil fertility and health is highly respected. Through their digestive processes, earthworms—especially species like Eisenia fetida—play a vital role in the vermicomposting process by consuming organic debris and changing it. Earthworms secrete digestive enzymes that facilitate the breakdown of complex organic substances into simpler forms, hence increasing the accessibility of key nutrients for plant absorption. Furthermore, this approach produces vermicompost that has a well-balanced nutritional profile, high in potassium, phosphorus, nitrogen, and other micronutrients. Earthworm-facilitated microbial activity also helps to improve soil structure, aeration, and water retention in general.

Another essential method for producing organic fertilizer is aerobic decomposition. With this process, organic compounds are broken down in the presence of oxygen. Microorganisms such as bacteria and fungi play a vital part in this process by utilizing oxygen to metabolize organic molecules. Compost that is rich in humus is created when the organic matter goes through several biochemical changes during aerobic decomposition.

This compost improves soil structure and encourages good microbial activity in addition to being a valuable source of nutrients. Because anaerobic decomposition produces disagreeable scents, the aerobic nature of the decomposition process guarantees that the end product is free of these smells. In addition, aerobic decomposition makes it easier for vital nutrients to be retained in a form that is more nutrient-available to plants, which enhances soil health overall.

Unlike aerobic decomposition, anaerobic decomposition is a unique process for producing organic fertilizer. Anaerobic microorganisms like methanogenic bacteria are used in this technique to break down organic compounds in the absence of oxygen. Biogas is a significant by-product of anaerobic decomposition that contains the strong greenhouse gas methane. Digestate, which is the term for the by-product of anaerobic decomposition, can be used as an organic fertilizer with lots of nutrients. However, to reduce the amount of methane released into the atmosphere, anaerobic decomposition needs to be carefully managed. The generated methane can be captured and used by putting anaerobic digestion systems in place, which will help turn it into a renewable energy source. Although managing methane emissions can be difficult, anaerobic decomposition is a useful method for recovering organic waste and creating fertilizers with added nutrients.

In the manufacture of organic fertilizers, fermentation processes comprise a wide range of methods, including lactic acid fermentation and bokashi fermentation. Lactic acid fermentation is the process by which organic matter is transformed into compost by lactic acid bacteria. This technique works especially well at protecting nutrients and stopping the spread of dangerous diseases.

Conversely, bokashi fermenting is a specialty method that comes from Japan. It entails the use of efficient microorganisms (EM) to assist ferment organic waste. Bokashi, the final product, is a pre-compost material that can be added to the soil to increase its fertility.

Through the addition of vital nutrients and the encouragement of the growth of advantageous microbes, fermentation processes help to improve the health of the soil. These methods are acknowledged for their effectiveness in dissolving intricate organic molecules and enabling the prompt transformation of organic waste into beneficial fertilizer.

To sum up, organic fertilizer production techniques are essential for improving the fertility and health of the soil. By using earthworms' natural ability to decompose material, vermicomposting creates compost that is high in nutrients and has a balanced nutrient profile. Utilizing oxygen-dependent bacteria, aerobic decomposition produces humus-rich compost that enhances soil structure and nutrient availability. While methane is a consequence of anaerobic decomposition, it also provides a way to recycle organic waste into fertilizers that are richer in nutrients.

This highlights the significance of appropriate management to reduce environmental repercussions. Lactic acid and bokashi fermentation are two examples of fermentation methods that offer more ways to turn organic resources into useful fertilizers while encouraging the development of healthy microorganisms in the soil. Combining these many processes for producing organic fertilizer gives agriculture sustainable options that improve soil health, protect the environment, and increase overall agricultural productivity.

CHAPTER SIX
ELEMENTS AFFECTING FERTILIZER GRADE
Choosing Raw Materials:

The careful selection of raw materials is essential to the creation of organic fertilizer. The composition of the selected raw materials has an intrinsic bearing on the final fertilizer product's quality and efficacy. The organic matter, nutrient concentrations, and general material appropriateness for the particular soil and crop needs must all be taken into account. Compost, plant leftovers, and animal dung are just a few of the organic materials that are evaluated during the selection process. To create an organic fertilizer that is both balanced and efficient, it is essential to comprehend the nutritional profiles and possible pollutants present in these raw materials. A thorough understanding of the local accessibility of these raw materials is also essential to guarantee an economical and sustainable production process.

Sufficient Maturation and Curing:

The production process of organic fertilizer undergoes crucial stages, namely curing and maturation, which have a substantial influence on its quality. Curing is the process of allowing organic materials to break down under controlled conditions so that complex molecules can more easily break down into simpler, nutrient-rich forms. The length of time and curing conditions—temperature and airflow, for example—have a significant impact on the stability and nutritional content of the finished fertilizer. In contrast, the stabilization of the cured material is referred to as maturation. This stage guarantees that the fertilizer is beneficial to soil health by reducing phytotoxic chemicals and increasing microbial activity. Optimizing nutrient availability and reducing the chance of nutrient loss through leaching or volatilization need a thorough understanding of the biological and chemical processes involved in curing and maturation.

Quality Control Measures:

Ensuring a consistent and dependable product during the production process of organic fertilizer necessitates the strict maintenance of quality control methods. Testing raw ingredients, keeping an eye on fermentation processes, and evaluating the finished product are just a few of the procedures that make up quality control. At every stage, meticulous testing is necessary to determine the nutrient content, microbial activity, and presence or absence of pollutants. This includes measuring nutrient levels and making sure that regulations are followed by using analytical methods like spectrophotometry and chromatography. Furthermore, microbiological investigations aid in determining whether beneficial bacteria and dangerous diseases are present. Putting in place strong quality control procedures not only protects the fertilizer's efficacy but also builds market credibility and cultivates confidence among farmers and other stakeholders.

Improving The Health Of The Soil:

Optimal Provision of Nutrients:

Organic fertilizers are essential for improving soil health because they supply the soil with a wide range of well-balanced nutrients. Organic fertilizers made from a variety of sources provide a more complete nutrient profile than synthetic fertilizers, which may have a restricted nutrient composition. A comprehensive approach to soil fertility is encouraged by the inclusion of secondary and micronutrients together with important components like potassium, phosphorus, and nitrogen. Maintaining plant growth, increasing crop yields, and avoiding nutrient imbalances or deficiencies—which can hurt the health of both soil and plants—all depend on achieving a balanced supply of nutrients.

Soil structure and microbial activity:

The capacity of organic fertilizers to promote beneficial microbial activity in the soil is one of their unique selling points. Microorganisms such as bacteria, fungi, and actinomycetes play a critical role in nutrient cycling and organic waste breakdown. By giving these microbes a substrate, organic fertilizers foster a dynamic and mutually beneficial relationship that increases soil fertility. Furthermore, by encouraging the development of aggregates, enhancing water retention, and lowering soil erosion, the organic matter in these fertilizers improves soil structure. Consequently, this fosters the growth of plant roots and makes it easier for gasses, nutrients, and water to pass between the soil and the roots of the plants.

Carbon Fixation and Organic Matter in Soils:

The process of sequestering carbon in the soil, which is facilitated by organic fertilizers, has significant implications for reducing the effects of climate change. These fertilizers' organic matter acts as a carbon sink, raising the amount of organic carbon in the soil. By lowering atmospheric carbon dioxide levels, this not only helps mitigate climate change but also improves soil health. An increase in soil organic matter enhances the soil's ability to retain nutrients, hold water, and structure. The long-term advantages of using organic fertilizers to sequester carbon highlight its significance for both environmental conservation efforts and sustainable agriculture.

Diminished Effect on the Environment:

Because organic fertilizer production reduces the environmental impact of conventional fertilizer use, it is consistent with sustainable farming methods. The chance of contaminating soil and water is reduced when organic fertilizers don't contain synthetic chemicals. Furthermore, the use of locally produced and renewable raw materials lowers the carbon impact of manufacture and shipping. Using organic fertilizers encourages the creation of a closed-loop system in which organic waste is converted back into beneficial soil nutrients. This not only helps with the problem of managing organic waste but also makes the agricultural ecosystem more sustainable and circular.

In summary, the creation of organic fertilizers and their use in farming are complex processes requiring careful consideration of the selection of raw materials, monitoring of the curing and maturation processes, and application of strict quality control procedures. The total effectiveness and quality of organic fertilizers are influenced by these parameters taken together. Moreover, the implementation of organic fertilizers aids in improving soil health by offering balanced nutrients, promoting microbial activity, encouraging carbon sequestration, and lessening environmental effects. The use of organic fertilizers is becoming more and more important in promoting resilient and healthy soils for coming generations as agriculture moves toward more sustainable and regenerative methods.

CHAPTER SEVEN
INNOVATIVE METHODS FOR PRODUCING ORGANIC FERTILIZERS

Utilizing Microbial Inoculants and Biofertilizers

Microbial inoculants and biofertilizers have become essential elements in improving soil health by producing organic fertilizers. These goods include a wide range of microorganisms that support soil nutrient availability and cycling, including fungi, bacteria, and algae. The primary idea behind the use of biofertilizers is to encourage biological processes that help plants absorb and mobilize nutrients. By developing symbiotic interactions with plant roots, these bacteria improve nutrient absorption and, as a result, crop yields.

Nitrogen-fixing bacteria are a well-known example of biofertilizers; they are essential for transforming atmospheric nitrogen into a form that plants can use. By reducing reliance on synthetic nitrogen fertilizers, the application of these microbial inoculants mitigates environmental risks related to their overuse. Furthermore, adding phosphorus-solubilizing microorganisms to organic fertilizers increases the amount of phosphorus that is available to plants. This all-encompassing method of managing soil fertility is in line with sustainable farming methods, encouraging a healthy ecosystem that is advantageous to crops as well as the environment.

Including Fungi From Mycorrhiza:

Mycorrhizal fungi are a sophisticated tactic used in the manufacture of organic fertilizers to improve soil health. Mycorrhizae associate with plant roots to develop mutualistic partnerships that increase the root system's reach and enhance its capacity to absorb nutrients. By functioning as an underground network, these fungi help plants and the soil exchange nutrients. Mycorrhizal fungi increase the efficiency of nitrogen uptake, which helps plants withstand a variety of stresses like drought and nutrient shortages.

Mycorrhizal fungi are essential for improving soil structure as well as nutrient uptake. Glomalin, a glycoprotein secreted by them, improves soil aggregation, which in turn helps retain water and stops soil erosion. Incorporating mycorrhizal fungus into organic fertilizers promotes plant health while also adding to the agriculture systems' overall sustainability. This creative method emphasizes the interdependence of biological processes in agriculture, which is in line with the tenets of agroecology.

Innovative Composting Technologies:

One important aspect of producing organic fertilizer is the use of advanced composting methods, which provide a long-term solution for waste management and nutrient recycling. In traditional composting, organic matter is broken down by microorganisms, creating humus-rich compost in the process. However, improvements in composting methods have produced more controlled and effective processes that optimize nutrient retention while reducing environmental impact.

Using aerobic composting systems, which employ the activity of microorganisms that require oxygen to speed up the breakdown process, is one such improvement. This technique preserves vital nutrients, which not only shortens the composting period but also improves the final product's quality. A nutrient-balanced organic fertilizer can also be made by combining a variety of organic inputs, including green waste, animal dung, and agricultural leftovers.

An additional level of innovation is added to the manufacture of organic fertilizers by utilizing specialist composting technologies like thermophilic and vermicomposting. Earthworms are used in vermicomposting to speed up decomposition and nutrient transformation, producing a vermicompost that is rich in nutrients. Conversely, high temperatures are necessary for thermophilic composting to accelerate the decomposition of organic matter and guarantee that pathogens and weed seeds are removed.

By encouraging sustainable waste management techniques, these cutting-edge composting systems not only provide superior organic fertilizers but also address environmental issues.

In conclusion, a paradigm shift toward sustainable and regenerative agricultural methods is represented by the incorporation of biofertilizers, mycorrhizal fungi, and cutting-edge composting technology in the manufacture of organic fertilizer. In addition to improving soil health, these cutting-edge methods reduce agriculture's environmental impact while boosting crop resilience and yield. Adopting these ideas is essential as the world's agricultural landscape changes because it will promote a harmonious relationship between agriculture and the environment, which will guarantee food security and ecological sustainability for coming generations.

CHAPTER EIGHT

INCREASING PRODUCTION FOR COMMERCIAL USE

Comparing Large- And Small-Scale Production:

A thorough assessment of numerous variables is necessary when going from small- to large-scale organic fertilizer production to guarantee cost-effectiveness, efficiency, and adherence to sustainable principles. A few key characteristics of small-scale production are low output, rudimentary machinery, and human labor. On the other hand, to satisfy the demands of a larger market, large-scale production requires mechanization, cutting-edge technologies, and optimized procedures. A thorough understanding of the entire organic fertilizer production process, including the sourcing of raw materials, composting, and packaging, is necessary for scaling up. It is necessary to handle issues like preserving product quality and consistency while growing volume. Furthermore, large-scale production depends heavily on economies of scale, which affect prices, costs, and overall market competitiveness. The availability of resources, consumer demand, and the dedication to sustainable agricultural methods are some of the variables that affect how scalable the production of organic fertilizer can be.

Considerations For Facilities And Equipment:

The design of facilities and the use of suitable machinery are critical components of commercially viable organic fertilizer manufacturing. Evaluating the requirements of every stage of production, from handling raw materials to packing, is necessary when selecting the appropriate equipment. Modern pelletizers, drying systems, mixers, and composting equipment all help to increase productivity and shorten turnaround times. To achieve the best possible nutrient retention and microbial activity during the composting process, the machinery selection must take into account the properties of the organic materials being employed. Facilities should be planned to minimize contamination hazards, promote efficient workflow, and adhere to safety regulations. Enough storage must be provided for finished goods, by-products, and raw materials. Furthermore, it is critical to include technologies for environmental sustainability and waste management throughout the design phase. A well-equipped and creatively built plant not only improves production efficiency but also contributes to the overall quality and marketability of the organic fertilizer.

Compliance With Regulations And Accreditation:

Regulatory compliance and certification play a critical role in maintaining product quality, consumer confidence, and environmental sustainability as the organic fertilizer market grows. Respecting national and international laws is necessary to prevent legal issues and rejection from the market. Compliance entails adhering to regulations on acceptable chemicals, labeling, and product composition. A certification attesting to the observance of organic farming practices and principles is frequently given by organic certifying authorities. Strict documentation of production procedures, input materials, and inspection records is necessary for certification acquisition and maintenance. Customers are reassured by regulatory compliance and certification, which confirms the fertilizer's organic status and enhances soil health. Moreover, it creates a reputation in the agriculture industry and opens doors to larger markets. Long-term success in the organic fertilizer sector requires constant observation and adjustment to changing rules.

To sum up, the process of shifting from producing organic fertilizer on a small scale to a large-scale scale necessitates managing intricate issues of production volume, choice of machinery, and adherence to regulations. Efficiency and sustainability must be balanced, and every choice made during the scaling-up process has a big impact on the venture's final success. Meticulous planning and execution are essential for everything from the selection of machinery to facility design and certification procedures. Accepting these factors guarantees a strong basis for economic success as the organic fertilizer market expands, and it also advances the more general objectives of improving soil health and sustainable agriculture.

CHAPTER NINE

CASE STUDIES IN PROFITABLE ORGANIC FARMING

1 Outlining the Effect of Organic Fertilizer on Crop Yields

The effect of organic fertilizer, which comes from natural sources, on crop yields in contemporary agriculture has drawn a lot of attention. A common motivation for the move toward organic farming methods is the aim to reduce the negative effects on the environment and advance sustainable agriculture. The impact of organic fertilizers on agricultural production is one important factor. The usage of organic fertilizers is positively correlated with higher agricultural output, as numerous studies have shown. This effect can be linked to the varied nutrient makeup of organic fertilizers, which contain secondary and micronutrients in addition to important components like potassium, phosphorus, and nitrogen.

A steady and balanced supply of nutrients to crops is supported by the organic fertilizers' progressive release of nutrients, which promotes healthy plant growth and development.

Moreover, organic fertilizers enhance the soil's ability to retain water and its structure. Consequently, this improves the general efficiency of plant uptake of nutrients. In contrast to synthetic fertilizers, organic substitutes encourage healthy microbial activity in the soil in addition to providing vital nutrients. The symbiotic connection between soil microbes and organic fertilizers improves nutrient cycling, increasing the bioavailability of nutrients for plants.

These all-encompassing relationships demonstrate the complex effects of organic fertilizers on crop yields as well as their ability to support resilient and sustainable agricultural systems.

Addressing the environmental issues related to conventional farming systems requires agriculture to embrace sustainable practices. The manufacture of organic fertilizer is essential to encouraging sustainability in the agriculture industry. In contrast to synthetic fertilizers, organic substitutes are generally sourced from sustainable materials like animal dung, compost, and cover crops.

These substances are a byproduct of the regeneration cycle, which turns waste materials into useful agricultural inputs. In addition to lowering reliance on non-renewable resources, this closed-loop strategy lessens the environmental damage caused by the extraction and production of synthetic fertilizers.

Sustainable agricultural practices have many advantages for the environment, but they also take a comprehensive strategy that takes into account the social and economic aspects of farming communities. Purchasing ingredients locally is a common practice in the creation of organic fertilizer, which boosts local economies. Moreover, the decreased dependence on chemical inputs mitigates the possibility of soil deterioration and water contamination, preserving the agricultural land's long-term yield. The agricultural sector may move toward a more resilient and ecologically harmonious model that satisfies the requirements of the present without jeopardizing the ability of future generations to meet their own needs by adopting sustainable methods, such as the use of organic fertilizers.

Three Actual Cases of Improving Soil Health

Several case studies from real-world experiences demonstrate how applying organic fertilizers improves soil health and the transformative power of these sustainable practices. Farmers that switched to organic fertilizer-based methods have seen significant gains in soil fertility, structure, and general health in several different parts of the world. Reintroducing decomposed organic matter to the soil through the use of compost as an organic fertilizer is one prominent example. This improves soil structure and adds necessary nutrients while encouraging aeration and water infiltration.

Another organic farming technique that shows how a variety of plant species can improve soil health is cover crop rotations. By adding nitrogen-fixing legumes to these rotations, soil fertility is raised and the requirement for external nitrogen inputs is decreased. The favorable results shown in these actual situations highlight the ability of organic fertilizers to address problems with soil degradation and promote sustainable agricultural landscapes.

Additionally, using organic fertilizers has been linked to less of an adverse effect on the environment in terms of water pollution and greenhouse gas emissions. Because organic fertilizers don't include synthetic chemicals, there is less chance of nutrient runoff, protecting the water quality of surrounding ecosystems. These real-world instances provide useful examples of how organic fertilizers can enhance crop yields while also enhancing the general resilience and health of agricultural soils.

In conclusion, the ideas of demonstrating the influence of organic fertilizers on crop yields, sustainable agricultural methods, and actual cases of improving soil health all work together to highlight the revolutionary potential of organic fertilizers in contemporary agriculture. The favorable results shown in several case studies highlight the necessity of a paradigm change in favor of sustainable and regenerative farming methods that put the well-being of agricultural systems and the environment first. Adopting the concepts of organic fertilizer production is becoming more and more important as the world's agricultural landscape changes to ensure food security, environmental preservation, and the long-term survival of farming communities.

CHAPTER TEN

CROP MANAGEMENT SYSTEMS INTEGRATING ORGANIC FERTILIZERS

A key component of sustainable agriculture is the incorporation of organic fertilizers into crop management systems, to maximize environmental benefits while improving soil fertility and health. Organic fertilizers are vital for giving crops the nutrients they need without using artificial chemicals. They come from natural sources including compost, manure, and plant leftovers. This idea stresses a comprehensive method of farming that takes into account the connections between plants, soil, and the larger ecosystem. Farmers can use methods that support long-term soil sustainability and overall agricultural resilience by incorporating organic fertilizers.

Agricultural-Specific Fertilization Techniques:

One of the mainstays of organic farming systems is crop-specific fertilizing strategies. It is crucial to comprehend the subtle differences in nutrient requirements of crops at different stages of growth to maximize both yield and quality. Crop-specific fertilization strategies entail a careful examination of the nitrogen, phosphorous, potassium, and micronutrient contents of organic fertilizers. Farmers can efficiently correct deficiencies in their crops by applying organic fertilizer in a way that aligns with their unique demands. This minimizes the hazards associated with excess nutrient runoff and its effects on the environment. This accuracy in fertilizing promotes healthy crop development and maximizes resource efficiency, which adds to the overall success of organic agricultural systems.

Rotating crops and using cover crops:

Two essential techniques in organic farming that greatly improve soil health are crop rotation and cover crops. Crop rotation is the practice of switching up the crops cultivated in a particular field from one season to the next. This tactic minimizes soil-borne pathogens, breaks the cycles of disease and pests, and maximizes the use of nutrients.

Conversely, cover cropping is the practice of growing non-commercial crops in the fields when the primary cash crop is not being grown.

These cover crops improve the amount of organic matter in the soil, fix nitrogen, and stop soil erosion. When crop rotation and cover crops are used in tandem, agricultural ecosystems become more resilient overall, increase biodiversity, and have better soil structure when organic fertilizers are used.

How To Balance Other Inputs With Organic Fertilizers:

In organic agricultural systems, achieving a balanced supply of nutrients is essential, which calls for the careful blending of organic fertilizers with other inputs. Although organic fertilizers are a useful source of nutrients, they cannot always fully satisfy crop requirements. To fill in any nutritional deficiencies, a comprehensive strategy combines organic fertilizers with additional inputs like mineral amendments or biofertilizers.

To maximize the synergy between organic and extra inputs, this notion highlights the significance of soil testing and nutrient management planning. Achieving the ideal balance between preventing over-application, which can result in nutrient imbalances or environmental pollution, and ensuring that crops receive enough nutrients for maximum growth. This integrative method emphasizes a harmonious interaction between natural processes and agricultural productivity, which is in line with the tenets of organic agriculture.

In summary, the goal of integrating organic fertilizers into crop management systems is to improve soil health through a multidimensional strategy. Crop rotation, cover crops, crop-specific fertilizing techniques, and the careful balancing of organic fertilizers with other inputs all help to maintain the resilience and sustainability of agricultural ecosystems.

Farmers may maximize nutrient management, lessen their impact on the environment, and support the long-term sustainability of organic agricultural systems by implementing these methods.

CHAPTER ELEVEN

ECONOMIC AND ENVIRONMENTAL ADVANTAGES OF ORGANIC FERTILIZERS

Diminished Effect On The Environment:

The manufacture of organic fertilizer is essential to reducing the negative environmental effects of conventional farming operations. The lower chance of soil and water pollution is one of the main benefits. Organic fertilizers come from natural sources such as plant materials, animal dung, and compost, as opposed to chemical fertilizers. Because of its natural organic makeup, there is less chance that poisons and dangerous manmade substances may enter the water and soil ecosystems. Consequently, using organic fertilizers helps save aquatic life and maintains the quality of the water. Additionally, organic fertilizers promote a better and more sustainable interaction between plants and the environment by facilitating nutrient cycling within the soil. This decrease in environmental effects promotes long-term ecological equilibrium and is consistent with the ideas of sustainable agriculture.

Organic Farming And Its Ability To Make Money:

Beyond the short-term advantages of increased crop yield, organic farming has many other benefits that contribute to its economic viability. The production of organic fertilizer, which has several benefits, is a crucial component of this economic paradigm. First off, producers can save money by using less costly synthetic fertilizers, which is one of the benefits of organic farming. The long-term advantages of producing organic fertilizer, such as increased soil fertility and less reliance on outside inputs, offset the possibly higher initial cost. This leads to ongoing cost-effectiveness. Furthermore, crop rotation and diversification are key components of organic farming systems, which reduce the chance of pest and disease outbreaks. Thus, less expensive chemical interventions are required, increasing overall farm profitability. Furthermore, there are increasing market prospects for farmers using organic practices due to the growing demand for produce farmed organically. Thus, organic farming's economic viability—which is bolstered by the use of organic fertilizer—underlines its potential as a robust and financially sustainable agricultural strategy.

The generation of organic fertilizer is essential to maintaining biodiversity and advancing the general health of ecosystems. Using organic fertilizers encourages a more varied and well-balanced microbial life in the soil. Because of the increased nutrient cycling caused by this microbial diversity, plants have easier access to vital components. Consequently, the soil transforms into a flourishing environment for an extensive variety of advantageous creatures, such as fungi, earthworms, and bacteria, all of which are essential for preserving the fertility and structure of the soil. Promoting biodiversity affects the entire agroecosystem, not just the soil.

By promoting natural insect predators through the use of organic fertilizers, organic farming methods lessen the need for chemical pesticides that may endanger non-target species. This all-encompassing method of farming recognizes the connection between ecology and agriculture, in line with the tenets of agroecology. The creation of organic fertilizer enhances ecosystem health and biodiversity, bolstering agricultural landscape resilience and sustainability.

To sum up, the manufacture of organic fertilizer presents a comprehensive approach to addressing the environmental and financial difficulties linked to traditional farming methods. By minimizing their negative effects on the environment, maintaining economic feasibility, and promoting ecosystem health and biodiversity, organic fertilizers aid in the growth of resilient and sustainable agricultural systems. The need for sustainable methods of producing food is growing worldwide, and one way to improve soil health is by using organic fertilizers. The move toward sustainable and organic farming is a revolutionary strategy that is consistent with the values of long-term ecological balance and conscientious resource management.

CHAPTER TWELVE

OVERCOMING OBSTACLES IN THE ADOPTION OF ORGANIC FERTILIZERS

The adoption of organic fertilizer in contemporary agriculture techniques is hampered by several issues. The ubiquity of myths and misconceptions about organic fertilizers is one major barrier. These false beliefs are frequently the result of ignorance or incomplete knowledge regarding the advantages and efficacy of organic fertilizers in comparison to synthetic ones. Farmers and other interested parties might think that organic fertilizers are less effective or don't contain enough nutrients to support healthy crop growth. Promoting the use of organic fertilizers requires addressing common misconceptions.

Research institutes and agricultural extension services are essential in distributing factual information to dispel these myths. It is important to use data-driven facts and scientific studies to show how effective organic fertilizers are at improving soil health and advancing sustainable agriculture. Stakeholders can actively engage with farmers by arranging workshops, seminars, and awareness campaigns, equipping them with the essential knowledge to make well-informed decisions regarding the use of organic fertilizers.

Farmer And Consumer Education

Education emerges as a cornerstone in the successful application of organic fertilizer systems. Farmers should be knowledgeable about the advantages of organic fertilizers and their ability to improve soil health because they are important decision-makers in the agriculture industry. A focused education strategy should include courses that explore the fundamentals of organic farming and emphasize the long-term benefits of applying organic fertilizers, such as increased crop quality, less environmental effects, and improved soil fertility.

In addition to learning how to apply organic fertilizers correctly, farmers should also learn how to incorporate organic farming methods into their entire crop management plans. Crop rotation, cover crops, and other environmentally friendly methods that complement organic fertilizers are included in this. Additionally, through their purchasing decisions, customers have a significant influence on agricultural methods. Demand-driven shifts toward organic produce can be achieved by informing consumers about the advantages that crops cultivated with organic fertilizers have for the environment and human health.

Institutional And Governmental Assistance

The backing of organizations and political authorities is crucial to the use of organic fertilizer. Governments have the power to significantly increase the use of organic fertilizers by providing funds for research, subsidies, and legislative frameworks.

The widespread use of organic fertilizers can be greatly increased by putting rules in place that support sustainable agriculture and offering financial incentives to farmers who adopt organic practices.

Research organizations and agricultural universities support this process by creating new technologies, offering extension services, and carrying out in-depth analyses on the efficacy of organic fertilizers. These organizations ought to work together with farmers and other industry participants to close the gap that exists between scientific understanding and real-world application. In addition, the implementation of certification schemes for organic goods guarantees the genuineness and excellence of organic fertilizers, thereby fostering trust among farmers and consumers.

overcoming the obstacles to the widespread use of organic fertilizer necessitates a multipronged strategy that dispels myths, informs important players, and wins over institutional and governmental support.

By dismantling myths, providing comprehensive education, and fostering a supportive policy environment, the agricultural sector can transition towards sustainable practices that enhance soil health and contribute to the long-term well-being of the environment and society.

CHAPTER THIRTEN
PROSPECTS FOR THE PRODUCTION OF ORGANIC FERTILIZERS

Emerging technologies that have the potential to completely transform the sector are driving breakthroughs in the manufacture of organic fertilizer in the future. The incorporation of precision agricultural methods into organic farming practices is one trend worth mentioning.

To maximize the usage of organic fertilizers, precision agriculture makes use of data-driven technologies like sensor-equipped drones and GPS-guided tractors. This strategy reduces waste and its negative effects on the environment by ensuring that nutrients are administered exactly where they are needed.

Investigating innovative microbial-based organic fertilizers is another exciting direction. Beneficial microbes have a critical role in soil health, according to research in microbial ecology. Harnessing these bacteria for organic fertilizer formulations might boost nutrient availability and promote plant development. In addition, there is increased interest in the creation of fertilizers based on biochar.

In addition to sequestering carbon, biochar—a carbon-rich substance generated from organic sources—also enhances soil structure and nutrient retention, all of which support long-term soil health.

Investigation And Advancement In Organic Farming:

Developments in organic agricultural research and development are closely related to the advancements in the manufacturing of organic fertilizers. Innovative strategies to maximize nutrient cycling in organic systems are being actively investigated by the scientific community. Improving nutrient utilization efficiency by using slow-release organic fertilizers is one area of focus. These formulations minimize nutrient leaching while meeting plant needs by releasing nutrients gradually over an extended period.

Furthermore, the creation of sustainable organic fertilizer is being aided by technological developments in the recycling of organic waste. Scientists are investigating methods for effectively turning organic waste—such as leftover crops and kitchen scraps—into composts and organic amendments that are high in nutrients.

This offers a useful source of organic matter to improve soil fertility in addition to addressing the waste management issue.

Organic Fertilizers' Place in Sustainable Agriculture

Because organic fertilizers solve the ecological and environmental issues related to conventional farming practices, they are essential in fostering sustainable agriculture. Mitigating soil deterioration by enhancing soil fertility and structure is a crucial component. The application of organic fertilizers, especially those enhanced with organic matter, can minimize soil erosion and promote long-term soil health by improving soil aggregation, water retention, and microbial activity.

Furthermore, using organic fertilizers helps to lessen agriculture's environmental impact by reducing the need for synthetic inputs. Because organic fertilizers don't include synthetic chemicals, there is less chance of groundwater contamination and nutrient runoff, which improves water quality. This move toward more environmentally friendly farming methods is in line with international programs to reduce global warming and protect biodiversity.

CONCLUSION

To sum up, the future of organic fertilizer manufacturing is bright, with new technologies showing promise, continuous research and development, and organic fertilizers playing a crucial role in supporting sustainable agriculture. The application of biochar, the investigation of microbial fertilizers, and precision agriculture are examples of how organic farming methods are being advanced. Research is being done in parallel to improve nutrient cycling, create slow-release formulations, and use organic waste to produce fertilizer sustainably.

It is impossible to exaggerate the importance of organic fertilizers in fostering soil health. Their value in sustainable agriculture is highlighted by their role in promoting a balanced environment, reducing degradation, and improving soil structure. Adopting organic fertilizers becomes a critical tactic as global agriculture struggles to feed a growing population while limiting its negative effects on the environment.

In the overall context of sustainable agriculture, the development of organic fertilizer production is evidence of the dedication to ecologically sound and environmentally friendly farming methods.

The future agricultural landscape will be shaped in large part by the ongoing cooperation of academics, farmers, and policymakers; this will put soil health, environmental sustainability, and the welfare of future generations first.